FLYING SNAKE

BRITTANY CANASI

Special Consultant
DR. JAKE SOCHA

Rourke
Educational Media
rourkeeducationalmedia.com

WORLD'S
COOLEST
SNAKES

Fast Facts

Family: Colubridae

Genus: *Chrysopelea*

Number of species: 5

Species: *Chrysopelea ornata, Chrysopelea paradisi, Chrysopelea pelias, Chrysopelea rhodopleuron, Chrysopelea taprobanica*

Diet: lizards, birds, rodents, bats

Range: Nepal, Bangladesh, Vietnam, Cambodia, Laos, Maluku, Thailand, Malaysia, China, Singapore, Indonesia, Burma, Philippines, India, and Sri Lanka

Table of Contents

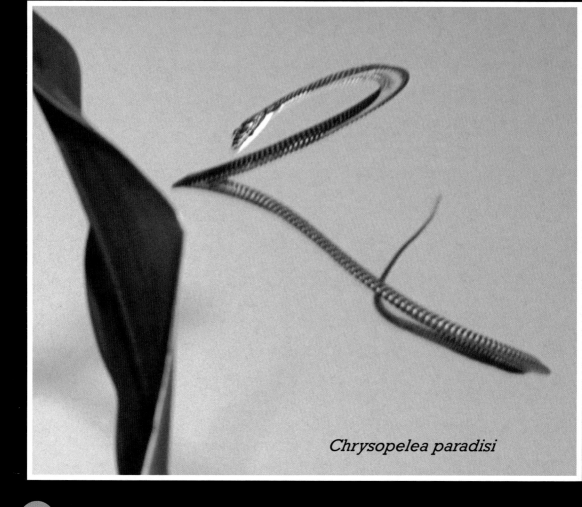

Chrysopelea paradisi

Flying snakes are venomous, but their venom is only dangerous to small prey. The venom likely wouldn't hurt anything bigger than a lizard.

Scary Stuff!

A fear of snakes is called *ophidiophobia*. A fear of flying animals is called *aerozoophobia*. Imagine having both and coming across a flying snake in the wild!

If this snake is on the ground, it's probably hiding out in bushes or ground-covering greenery. They mostly live in trees, though. That's where they travel best.

Reach for the Sky
The higher up on a tree a snake can climb, the farther it can glide.

Why call it gliding flight and not pure flying? When the flying snake takes off, it doesn't gain any **altitude**, or height. As it moves down, it can only go forward or turn to the side.

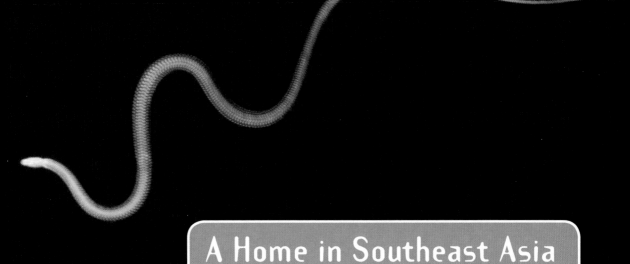

A Home in Southeast Asia
Flying snakes are found from western India to the Indonesian archipelago.

A flying snake just after takeoff.

Scientists aren't sure why the flying snake glides. It's possible it glides to hunt prey, avoid predators, and travel from tree to tree without having to touch the ground.

Smaller snakes can glide farther. Some can glide up to 99 feet (30.2 meters) when starting from 49 feet (15 meters) up. That's longer than two school buses parked end-to-end.

Meet the Fleet

There are five **species** of flying snakes. Some of them, like the Moluccan flying snake (*Chrysopelea rhodopleuron*) and the Sri Lankan flying snake (*Chrysopelea taprobanica*), are less studied than the others.

Don't Take Us Home

Flying snakes do not make great pets for most people. They require a hot and humid environment, and it's a plus if they have space to glide as they would in the wild. Some species can also be aggressive, and they are best kept in **captivity** by experienced caregivers only.

Sri Lankan flying snake – a rare find.

The golden tree snake, or the ornate flying snake, is the biggest of the five. It can grow up to about four feet (1.2 meters) long. Because of its size, it isn't the best glider.

Despite its name, it's not always gold. Sometimes it can have green, orange, or red markings.

Chrysopelea ornata

The belly scales form an edge, helping with grip.

Fact or Fiction?

The golden tree snake is only found in trees and bushes.

FICTION! Golden tree snakes have been found in thatched roofs in Thailand, preying on mice or geckos.

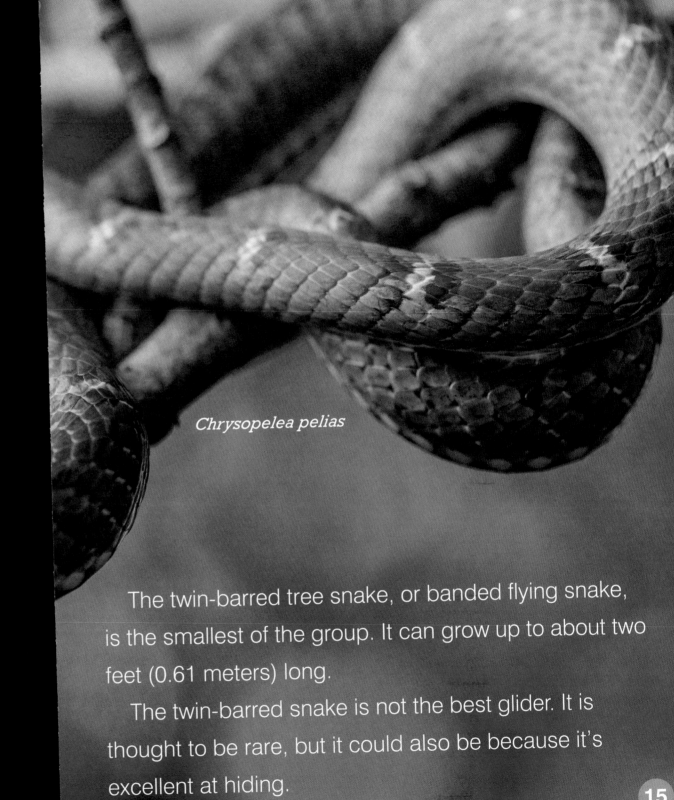

Chrysopelea pelias

The twin-barred tree snake, or banded flying snake, is the smallest of the group. It can grow up to about two feet (0.61 meters) long.

The twin-barred snake is not the best glider. It is thought to be rare, but it could also be because it's excellent at hiding.

Chrysopelea paradisi

The paradise tree snake grows to be about two or three feet (0.6 to 0.9 meters) long.

The best glider is the paradise tree snake. It's usually black and green, but some have red, orange, and yellow highlights.

The paradise tree snake can glide farther than the twin-barred tree snake or the golden tree snake. The Moluccan flying snake and the Sri Lankan flying snake have not been measured.

◀◀ *The red or orange petal pattern only occurs in some animals.*

Chrysopelea paradisi

Flight Manual

A flying snake's body is specifically designed to climb trees and glide from them. The design of a flying snake's body is specialized for flight.

The snake flattens its belly so it's more **aerodynamic**, almost doubling its original width. When it's not gliding, the scales on its belly help it move up trees and along branches.

To take off or jump, the snake slithers to the edge of the branch so that most of its body is hanging. It angles itself to aim for the direction it wants to glide. And then: liftoff.

Fact or Fiction?

Shape matters when it comes to flight.

FACT! The body shape of the flying snake changes to a triangle shape. Like a Frisbee, the air flowing on top and underneath helps create lift.

Shape of flying snake in flight

The snake propels off the branch and slithers in a **serpentine**, or snake-like, motion while midair to control the direction of the glide and land safely. Slithering in midair can help its **trajectory**, or flight path, as well. This is different from other gliding animals, like the flying squirrel or some lizards. They maintain the same shape during flight.

Tim Laman, professional photographer

Quite a Flight

Scientists used video cameras to study the flight of the paradise tree snake. They found that it achieved a 13-degree trajectory on its best trip. If it jumped off a 31.5-foot (9.6 meter) perch and flew at a 13-degree angle, it would land 69 feet (21 meters) away from the tree's base.

Dr. Jake Socha with his students in Singapore

On-Board Meals

The flying snake is **diurnal**, so it hunts in the daytime. It eats whatever it can find in trees, including lizards, rodents, birds, and bats.

To stun its prey, the flying snake uses its venomous fangs, which are in the back of its mouth. They are only about 1/10th of an inch (0.25 centimeters) long.

A golden tree snake eats a bat.

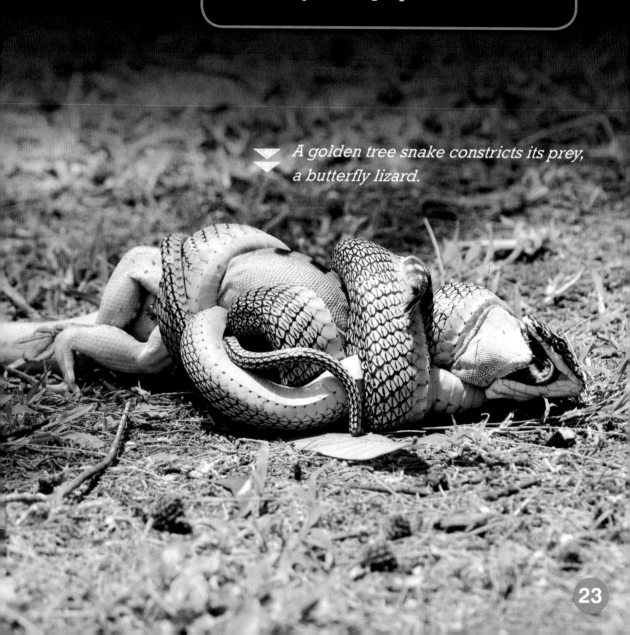

The flying snake can also kill its prey by constricting, or squeezing.

FACT! This snake's venom alone does not usually kill its prey.

A golden tree snake constricts its prey, a butterfly lizard.

Not much is known about what feeds on the flying snake. But because of their size and relatively weak venom, it's possible larger snakes like the king cobra could be a predator.

They also have to watch out for birds of prey such as great horned owls and buzzards.

king cobra

The Malayan water monitor, a large lizard, eats flying snakes.

great horned owl

Future Flyers

The female flying snake is **oviparous**, so she lays eggs shortly after they're fertilized.

C. paradisi eggs

She lays about six to twelve eggs at a time, and the eggs take about 90 days to hatch.

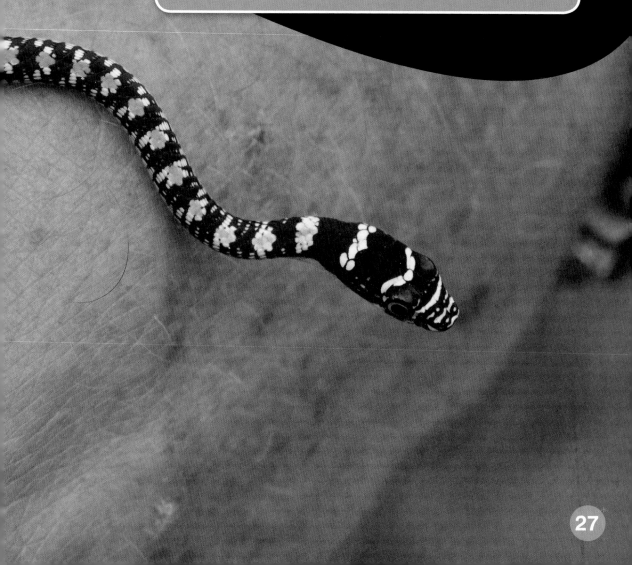

Tiny Gliders

Baby flying snakes are four to six inches (10 to 15 centimeters) long when they hatch. That's about the size of a pen!

The Science of Flight

The flying snake fascinates scientists. Not many animals are able to transform their entire body shape to fit one purpose, then change it back to fit another.

Scientists look to the flying snake to one day build a robot like it. Imagine if a robot could slither, wrap itself around things, fit into small spaces, and then glide from one spot to another. It could explore dangerous terrain, help with rescue missions, and even be used for medical procedures!

Glossary

aerodynamic (air-OH-dye-nam-ik): able to move through air very easily and quickly

altitude (AL-ti-tood): the height of something above the ground or above sea level

captivity (kap-TIV-i-tee): the condition of being held or trapped by people

diurnal (dye-UR-nuhl): of or belonging to the daytime

genus (JEE-nuhs): in taxonomy, a group of related plants or animals that is larger than a species but smaller than a family

oviparous (oh-VIP-er-uhs): producing eggs that mature and hatch after leaving the body

serpentine (SUR-puhnt-een): of or resembling a snake

species (SPEE -seez or SPEE -sheez): one of the groups into which animals and plants of the same genus are divided

trajectory (truh-JEK-tuh-ree): the curve described by a projectile, rocket, or similar object in its flight

Index

Show What You Know

1. How can the flying snake glide so well?
2. Why does the flying snake glide?
3. Where are flying snakes usually found?
4. Why are scientists so interested in studying the flying snake?

Further Reading

Arnold, Ted, *Fly Guy Presents: Snakes*, Scholastic, 2016.

Rajczak, Kristen, *How Snakes and Other Animals Taste the Air*, Rosen, 2016.

Alinsky, Shelby, *National Geographic Readers: Slither, Snake!*, National Geographic Children's Books, 2015.

Dr. Jake Socha's website: www.flyingsnake.org

About the Author

Brittany Canasi's job is in cartoons, and her passion is in writing. She has a B.A. in Creative Writing from Florida State University. If she could be any snake, it would be the flying snake, because it sounds like a better way to travel than driving. She lives in Los Angeles with her husband and very scruffy dogs.

Meet The Author!
www.meetREMauthors.com

Dr. Socha's research on flying snakes has been supported by Virginia Tech, the National Science Foundation (grant 1351322), DARPA, and the National Geographic Society. For more information, see: **www.flyingnake.org** and **www.thesochalab.org.**

www.rourkeeducationalmedia.com

PHOTO CREDITS: photography by Dr. Jake Socha expect for pg 5 ©Bob_Eastman, pg 10 ©Gihan Jayaweera, Pg 14-15 ©Chien C. Lee, pg 22 ©By Mrs–ya, pg 23 ©By Butterfly Hunter, pg 24 ©GlobalP, pg 24 ©Ed Brown Wildlife / Alamy Stock Photo, pg 25 ©ca2hill

Edited by: Keli Sipperley & Dr. Jake Socha
Cover & interior design by: Kathy Walsh

Library of Congress PCN Data

Flying Snake / Brittany Canasi
 (World's Coolest Snakes)
  ISBN 978-1-64156-484-7 (hard cover)
  ISBN 978-1-64156-610-0 (soft cover)
  ISBN 978-1-64156-723-7 (e-Book)
Library of Congress Control Number: 2018930703

Rourke Educational Media
Printed in the United States of America,
North Mankato, Minnesota